Color the Promises of God

Artwork by Lori Siebert

HARVEST HOUSE PUBLISHERS
EUGENE, OREGON

Design and production by Harvest House Publishers, Inc.

Cover by Katie Brady Design

COLOR THE BIBLE is a registered trademark of The Hawkins Children's LLC. Harvest House Publishers, Inc., is the exclusive licensee of the federally registered trademark COLOR THE BIBLE.

COLOR THE PROMISES OF GOD
Copyright © 2016 by Lori Siebert
Published by Harvest House Publishers
Eugene, Oregon 97402
www.harvesthousepublishers.com

ISBN 978-0-7369-6835-5

Printed in the United States of America

18 19 20 21 22 23 / ML-JC / 11 10 9 8 7 6 5

A Good Place to Begin

This coloring book is for artists of all ages and talents, and that means you! Let your creative spirit free, choose any color you like, and make each beautiful image your own. There are no rules except to have fun.

Enjoy the process. Feel free to use colored pencils, pens, water colors, markers, and crayons—or any combination thereof—to add color and texture to each design. Notice that all the pictures are printed on just one side of the paper. To keep colors from bleeding through to the next page, simply slip an extra piece of paper underneath the page you're working on. When finished, you might like to remove the page from the book, trim it to size, and frame your artwork for all to see.

Most importantly, have fun with the process. Enjoy experimenting with contrasting colors or different shades of the same color. Try lighter hues for a softer look or layer and blend your colors for even more options. Allow some white space or saturate the entire piece with rich vibrant color, depending on your mood. Let your worries go, relax in the moment, and allow your creative spirit to lead the way!

My PRESENCE will go WITH you, AND I will give You rest. —Exodus 33:14

COME to ME, all you who are WEARY and BURDENED, AND I will give you REST. —MATTHEW 11:28

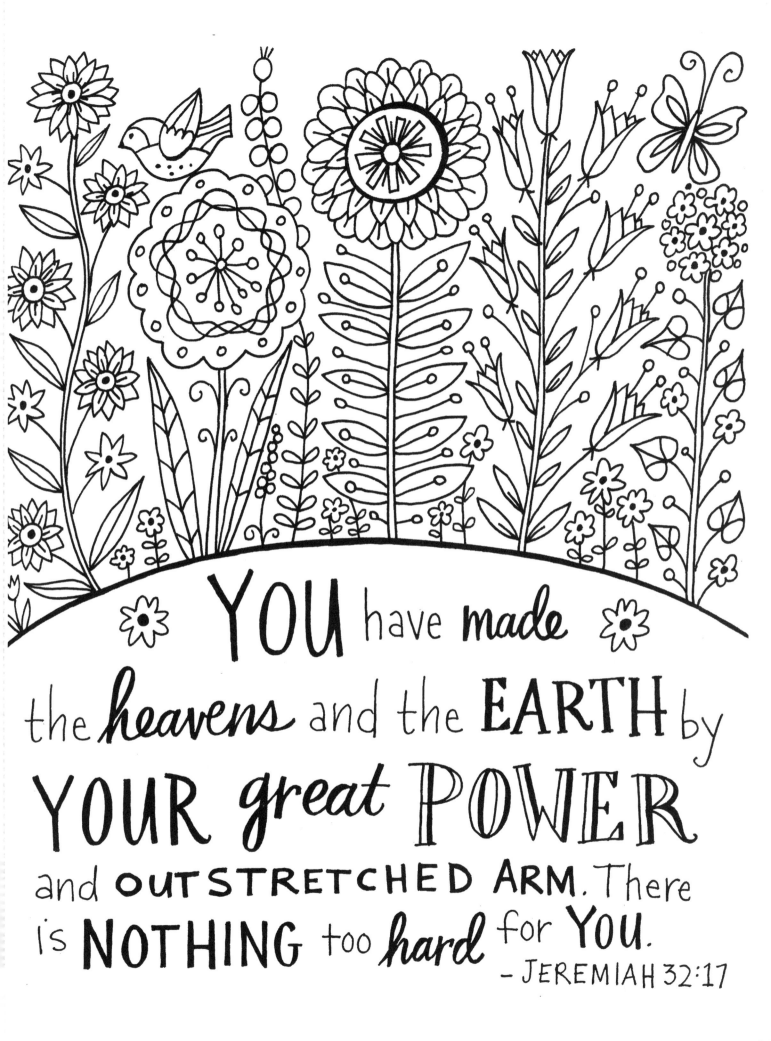

The LORD is near to ALL who CALL on HIM, to ALL who CALL on HIM in TRUTH

-Psalm 145:18

the Lord COMFORTS HIS PEOPLE.

ISAIAH 49:13

I will *counsel* you with my *loving* eye on *you.*
—PSALM 32:8

You will SEEK ME and FIND ME when you SEEK ME with ALL your heart. —Jeremiah 29:13

For as in ADAM all die,

So in Christ all will be made ALIVE.

1 -CORINTHIANS 15:22

He † is good... for His loving kindness is everlasting.
— 1 Chronicles 16:34

the Lord is GOOD to all; He has compassion on ALL HE has made.

— PSALM 145:9

my GOD will meet all your NEEDS according to the RICHES of his GLORY in Christ Jesus. -Philippians 4:19

love

cast ALL YOUR ANXIETY on HIM...

because HE cares for YOU.

1 Peter 5:7

Philippians 4:13

I CAN DO
ALL things
through HIM who
STRENGTHENS me.

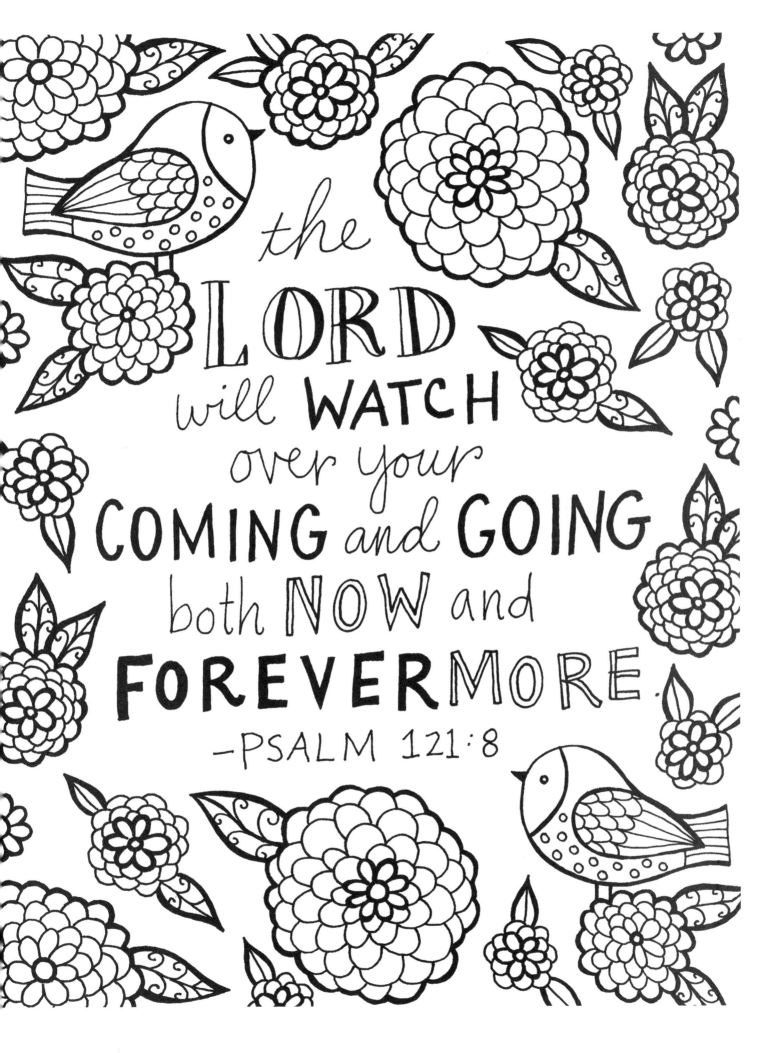

the LORD will WATCH over your COMING and GOING both NOW and FOREVERMORE.

—PSALM 121:8

If anyone is in CHRIST, the new creation has come: The old has gone, the new is HERE!

2 CORINTHIANS 5:17

the Lord Remembers us AND will BLESS us.

-PSALM 115:12

He will COVER You with HIS feathers, and UNDER HIS Wings You will FIND Refuge.

PSALM 91:4

I have LOVED You with an EVERLASTING Love

—JEREMIAH 31:3

Delight yourself in the LORD and HE will give you the desires of your HEART.
-PSALM 37:4

the LORD directs the steps of the GODLY. He *delights* in EVERY DETAIL of their LIVES.

—PSALM 37:23

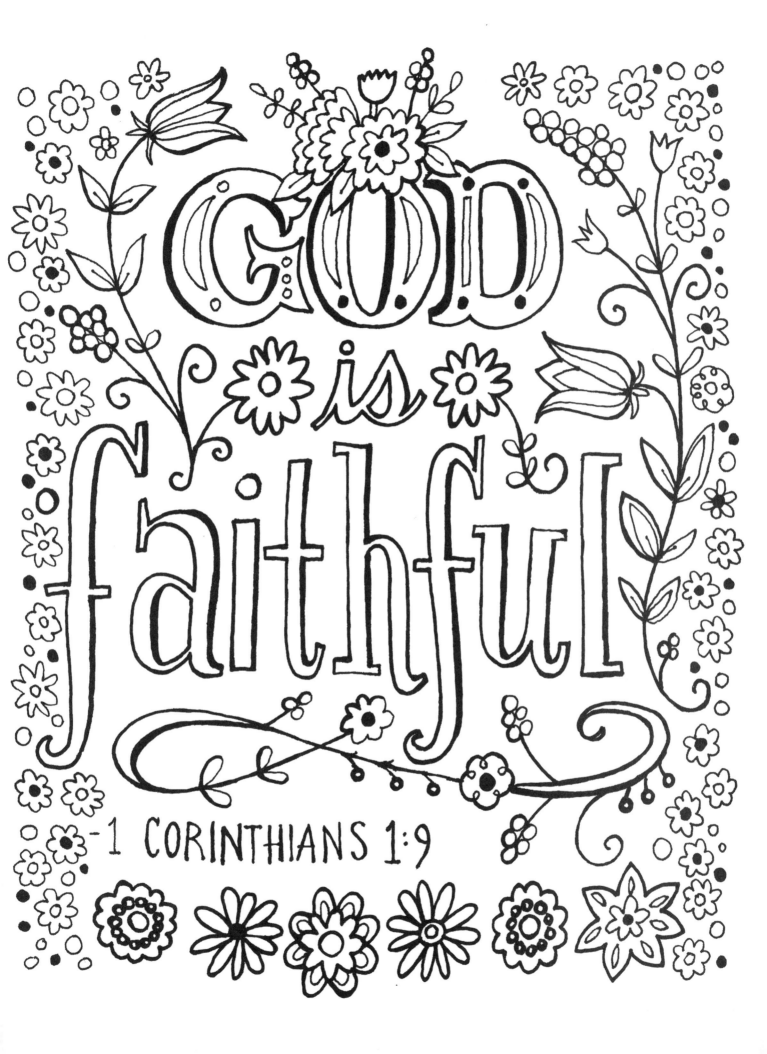

GOD is faithful

-1 CORINTHIANS 1:9

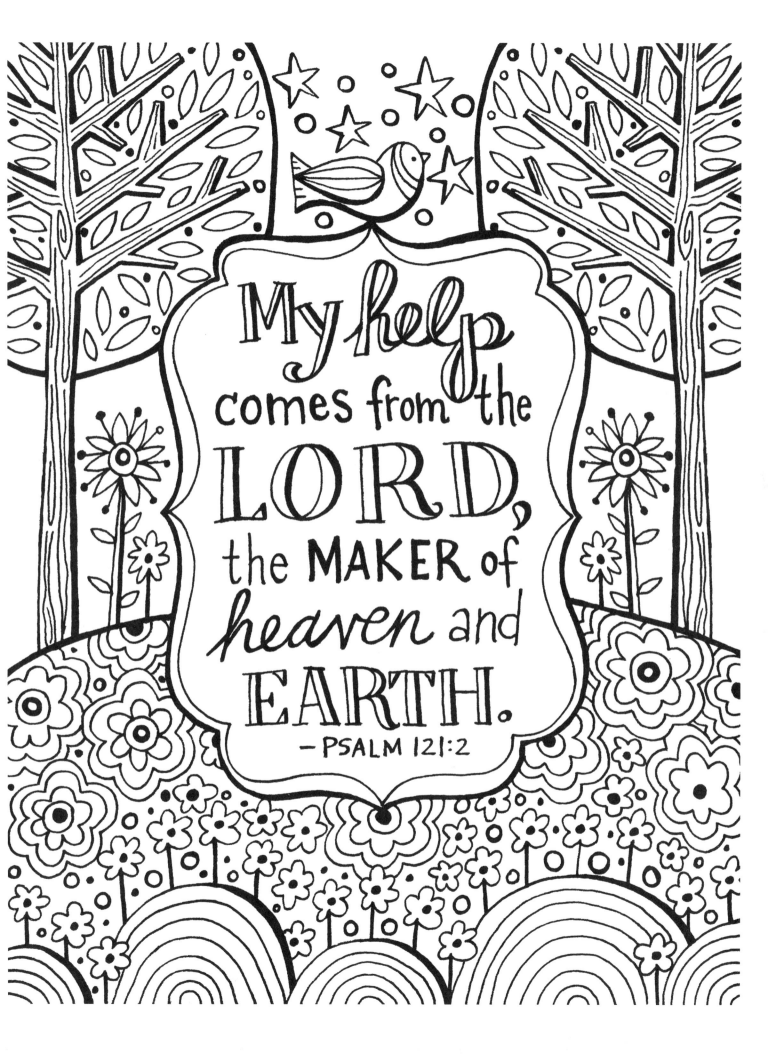

You both Precede and FOLLOW me and PLACE your hand of BLESSING on my HEAD.

—PSALM 139:5

About Lori Siebert

With an ever-expanding portfolio overflowing with originality, Lori Siebert started art lessons at age seven, then earned a degree in graphic design, and now has artwork featured in several books, including *101 Inspirational Thoughts to Brighten Your Day* and *The Friendship Garden*. She divides her time between sewing, sculpting, drawing, painting, and designing new products.

We'd love to see your creations!
Share your finished projects on social media with the hashtag

#colorthebible

We'll be looking for your artwork!

For information on more
Harvest House coloring books for adults, please visit
www.harvesthousepublishers.com

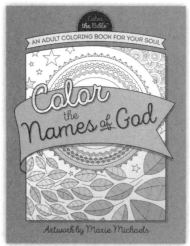